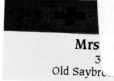

TALES *of* GRACE

Reflections on the Joyful Mysteries

By Luigi Santucci
Translated by Demetrio S. Yocum

PARACLETE PRESS
BREWSTER, MASSACHUSETTS

2015 First printing

Tales of Grace: Reflections on the Joyful Mysteries

English translation copyright © 2015 by Demetrio S. Yocum
Illustrations copyright © 2015 by George Kordis

ISBN 978-1-61261-639-1

Library of Congress Cataloging-in-Publication Data

Santucci, Luigi.
  [Misteri gaudiosi. English]
  Tales of grace : reflections on the Joyful Mysteries / by Luigi Santucci ;
translated by Demetrio S. Yocum.
      pages cm
  Originally published in Italian under title: Misteri gaudiosi : Milano : Edizioni
Gentile, La rassegna d'Italia, 1946.
  Includes index.
  1. Mary, Blessed Virgin, Saint--Fiction. 2. Jesus Christ—Fiction. 3. Rosary—
Fiction. I. Title.
  PQ4841.A67M5713 2015
  853'.914—dc23   2015001503

10 9 8 7 6 5 4 3 2 1

Published by Paraclete Press
Brewster, Massachusetts
www.paracletepress.com

Printed in the United States of America

CONTENTS

FOREWORD

═══

If you could crush heaven into a map,
you may find two half-heavens.
Half will be joy and half will be glory.
—JOHN DONNE

ONE OF THE MOST SIGNIFICANT, yet brief, embodiments of the new protagonism of the Catholic laity and militant Catholic Church during the forties that in many ways paved the way for the much needed reforms of Vatican II, was that of a group of Italian intellectuals and writers who created in 1944 the Christian-oriented journal *L'Uomo*. Among the founders were the poets David Maria Turoldo and Luigi Santucci. After that short-lived yet remarkable experience, both writers would leave a profound mark on the development of Italian poetry and literature, as well as Christian thought, in the second half of the twentieth century. In particular, Luigi Santucci's *Meeting Jesus, A New Way to Christ*, published in English in 1971, remains to this day a superbly imaginative and poetic reinterpretation of the person and life of Christ based on the Gospels.

A powerful image of the mystery of Christ's salvation in Santucci's book that I hold particularly dear is that of the bowl of water that Christ used to wash his disciples' feet. Santucci writes that if he could keep some relic of Christ's passion he would choose that bowl of dirty water. He would then go around the world to wash the feet of those he would encounter in the streets, never looking above their ankles, and never at their faces, so he could not tell friend from foe. This way he could wash the feet of *everyone*: saints and popes, presidents and kings, beggars and drug addicts, arms merchants and atheists—in silence, and *until they understood*. After all, our job is not to decide whom to save, but whom to serve. Jesus teaches us to be completely undiscriminating in our judgment of others; we should serve all because Christ dies for all, which is ultimately the meaning of Eucharist.

Aptly compared to the writings of St. Francis of Assisi and Pope John XXIII for its simplicity and beauty, Santucci's *Meeting Jesus* is profoundly poetic. Emerging from those pages is a Christology that teaches us to find in our quotidian existence the divine mystery of salvation and redemption. It also tells us that we have been called to contemplate the face of God precisely in the dirt and grit of our chaotic human reality. In short, Santucci powerfully reminds us that, as Pierre Teilhard de Chardin once wrote: "we are not human beings trying to have a spiritual experience; rather, we are spiritual beings having a human experience," and that our human experience should be embraced in all its often disquieting reality.

The following reflections by Santucci on the joyful mysteries, brilliantly and scrupulously translated into English for the first time by Demetrio S. Yocum, and splendidly illustrated by George Kordis's icons, represent an even more direct message of acceptance of the divine call in our everyday experience. Through the narration and the poetic humanization of the key figures of Christ's incarnation and adolescence, Santucci, in the great apologetic tradition, questions our faith, in its most profound recesses. In the end, there is not one single biblical episode that cannot be retold and reread in a new light, and with a new faith and hope, in order to reveal the most compelling secret: to know and "touch" Christ ("with the heart and not with the hand" as Bernard of Clairvaux put it) is the supreme reality and ultimate goal of our human existence.

We generally tend to associate the joyful mysteries with the reciting of the rosary. For centuries these mysteries of our faith have been prayed and meditated upon with the help of prayer beads, and essentially through the repetitions of the Our Father and Hail Mary. As I mention in my book *The Mystery of the Rosary: Marian Devotion and the Reinvention of Catholicism*, the rosary soon became associated with innovative and highly adaptable meditative practices that made a vivid use of imagination when "picturing" the biblical episodes in the lives of Christ and Mary. Further, more than simply recalling past events, the practice of meditating the rosary was intended to welcome the arrival and the coming into presence of fundamental persons and realities in our human lives: the Virgin Mary, Christ, and the mysteries of our salvation. In short, the ultimate goal was to "shrink the distance" between Christ, Mary, and the ordinary events in our lives. Going beyond the more devotional aspects of such practice, Santucci makes a step further toward a theology, profoundly joyful, of these mysteries. It is a "practical" theology, aiming to bring transformation and renewal in the lives of people, and that is centered on two main elements: Jesus's injunction to become like children, and what Santucci defines as "Christ-euphoria."

Undoubtedly, Jesus's command to "change and become like children" (Matthew 18:3) has to do with humility, as the tradition tells us. However, I believe that it has a strong relation to self-abandonment in faith as well. To become like children means more than anything else to not overthink, to welcome and accept as true what we are told. We all know how ready and enthusiastic children are to embrace and believe in tales and the stories the grown ups tell them. This is precisely what Santucci invites us to do: believe in the good news of the Gospel, in the mysteries of faith, with the abandonment of the child who believes in fairy tales. After all, did Jesus not make storytelling his preferred means of communication to teach us about God and the kingdom of heaven? What are the beatitudes and the parables if not wonderfully entertaining short stories of the greatest poetic mind? Jesus knew well that his teaching could not have been effective unless addressing first our imaginative faculties.

Santucci's storytelling, therefore, reminds us that we can discover the joys of the Gospels only if we accept them wholeheartedly and imaginatively—like a child would do. It then becomes our task, and our joy, to *retell* them again and again, to ourselves first, and then to others. And since the Gospels were written for us, so we would know what God the Father has in store for each one of us, our retelling necessarily will involve a great deal of imagination; an imagination that only children have, and that allows for a revolutionary and unique combination of biblical and personal experience in order to participate more fully to the joys of Christ's presence in our lives. "Let the little children come to me, and do not stop them; for it is to such as these that the kingdom of heaven belongs" (Matthew 19:14).

Santucci's unique and utterly delightful term "Christ-euphoria," denoting the sublime pleasures inherent in the newness of our Christian faith, is a spiritual balm that heals and kindles our hopes in the renewal of our contemporary and often moribund churches. The message is simple: by grace we have been saved in Christ Jesus (Ephesians 2:8), and God's grace allows us to be new creatures ready to experience everything anew. To all the church leaders and legislators, good only at defining and reminding us of our sins, debts, and omissions, Santucci replies with the simple joys and beauty of the Gospel message: can we be sad if the groom has promised to be with us "until the end of time" (see Matthew 28:20)? The answer is clearly no. After all, as St. John of the Cross wrote: "In the evening of life, we will be judged by love alone." If only for this one insight, we are grateful to Demetrio S. Yocum and Paraclete Press, who have made Santucci's wonderful reflections available to a wider English readership. In so doing, they have truly brought to light a hidden gem.

—NATHAN D. MITCHELL
University of Notre Dame

EDITOR'S NOTE

READERS FAMILIAR WITH THE WORK OF AUTHORS such as Dante, Charles Dickens, Virginia Woolf, and Marcel Proust soon realize that, instead of being on a clearly delineated journey with a sure ending in sight, they are in reality up for plot twists and turns and abrupt changes in style, as well as intricate perspectives and points of view. These are all literary techniques that make the reading experience more an exciting adventure than a relaxed journey, as they mirror the beauty and complexity of life itself and challenge us to embrace more fully our own multifaceted nature and the contradictory world we inhabit. In the following pages, Luigi Santucci does something similar as he takes us on a voyage where we are offered the rare chance to experience the joyful mysteries from a broad spectrum of perspectives. In many ways, Santucci is here transposing in writing the meditative practice of putting oneself into the biblical scenes describing the lives of Christ and Mary in order to experience, in the narrative of our own lives, their comforting company. Further, by approaching these mysteries from multiple viewpoints, Santucci reminds us that the chapters of our lives exist across time and space as part of a larger narrative: that of human salvation.

The five chapters of *Tales of Grace* are therefore uniquely fashioned stories with shifting narrative voices. In the first chapter, dedicated to the mystery of the Annunciation, we find the narrator talking to an angel and then reciting the rosary. The second chapter, which focuses on the mystery of the Visitation, takes us back to Ein Karim and offers an enchanting look into the everyday life of Mary, Elizabeth, and Zechariah. As we progress along this chapter, we soon realize that the narrator has taken on a more participatory role as the biblical events are seen through the eyes of one of the minor characters in the story, namely the dairy boy. In the third chapter, the Nativity, the narrator imagines a heavenly banquet where the villains of the story—Herod, Pilate, and Judas—are portrayed as minor scoundrels who can no longer spoil the eternal celebration of Christ's birth. Once again, the narrator here gradually becomes a character within the story as he retrieves his role of dairy boy and then of Roman soldier. By the end of this chapter, we have been gradually carried to modern times with the description of scenes from the narrator's own childhood as well as his slow regression to the first moments of his life. As we reach the mystery of the Presentation at the Temple, in the fourth chapter, the narrator has turned into a "modern" Simeon, and the scene takes place in a modern-day church where a child is brought to be baptized and a miracle occurs. Finally, at the mystery of Finding the Child Jesus in the Temple, the narrator finds himself at his old boarding school, where he carries on a spirited dialogue with the priests who were his former school teachers, passionately pleading for them to grasp the true meaning of the gospel.

We owe a deep debt of gratitude to George Kordis whose beautiful artwork accompanies this multilayered narration and illustrates the long-awaited Savior's coming into the world. His icons also take us beyond, to what lies ahead for the Child who will lay down his life to redeem us all and then will rise in triumph.

Come now, and sit at the feet of this master storyteller as he recounts *Tales of Grace*.

—DEMETRIO S. YOCUM

AUTHOR'S NOTE
TO THE READER

⸻

I CONSIDER THIS IS A "MATURE" BOOK, which nevertheless belongs, and puts an end, to my youth: I wrote it four years ago (I was a little more than twenty). I say this because it seems to me that at that time we were all still very young. Now instead, after all that has been, I feel as if we have outgrown those days.

I am not saying this to implore leniency or to compel the reader to frame these pages as a juvenile yet mature experience in an attempt to better understand or accept what I wrote. For I do not consider this book, as they say, *passé*. However, on account of the insistence of judicious and wise friends, I would like to call your attention especially to two things.

First, I hope that the final chapter, about experiencing "happiness" in a Christian perspective, does not offend those who have suffered much in their lives. I also hope that they will be able to understand the ironic message of those pages, which should prevent them from judging that chapter too severely. After all, it cost me countless rewriting efforts. Never before have I tormented myself so much to find words that can exalt the joys and delights of Christianity. This was a sign that the "joke," if you will, on which I knew I still had to work to conclude this book was, I felt, in conflict with a solemnity dear to your heart and mine that had already begun (it was the eve of the feast of the Nativity of the Virgin). Given the topic, to pull it off would have required a perfection and excellence attributable only to the holiness of Saint Francis, or the genius of G. K. Chesterton: needless to say how much I lack in both holiness and perfection.

Second, I hope that some down-to-earth expressions and passages, which may sound too casual in dealing with holy figures, do not displease you too much. On the one hand, I drew on the straightforward and anti-puritan naturalism of the Scriptures (New and Old Testament), which has remained incorrupt throughout our religious literature up to the Reformation. On the other, it was my precise intention to humanize my characters to prove that it is impossible to disrespect them even when we imagine them among us, around a hearth, telling stories.

Perhaps the following pages will remind you of Alessandro Manzoni's famous remark: "a hodgepodge of

Mardi Gras and Good Friday." Nevertheless, I think that my book, all in all, is in line with the teachings of the gospel of Jesus Christ. This is important to me because I would never want to cause distress to anybody, including the clergy of course, and, contrary to the last words of this book, I am very afraid of hell. . . .

Finally, rather than repeating Martial's statement *Lasciva est nobis pagina vita proba est* (My words may err, but my life is honest), if possible I would like to affirm the opposite: . . . *nobis pagina proba est* (. . . my words are honest).

—LUIGI SANTUCCI

Time on earth is more glorious than a thousand eternities:
here I can prepare myself for the Lord,
there I will never be able to do so.

—ANGELUS SILESIUS

THE
ANNUNCIATION

Angelus est testis
ad me missus coelestis.
Processit ex me spes mea:
sed incredula manet Judea.

(Angel-proof was given,
to me sent down from heaven,
my hope from my womb proceeded:
but Judea incredulous never heeded.)

—ADAM OF ST. VICTOR

Loreto, April 1

T HAT YEAR, EASTER FELL ON APRIL 1. The nice weather had arrived ahead of time. It was almost hot, and some tourists, who were there visiting the House with me, had taken their jackets off, displaying their glorious shirts with the unswerving pleasure of the hard-working veteran who plants a flag in front of his porch. They had white, pink, blue striped collars, impeccably ironed, and showy suspenders.

The guide started to explain: "The legend has it, ladies and gentlemen, that. . . ." But not far away, a young fellow wearing glasses with incredibly thick lenses and spaghetti-like hair was ostentatiously competing against the tourists' guide, speaking with a voice (not low enough) about some daub (yet to him of great value) to a flock of squawking girls (there are always those who think that they have no need of a guide, even when visiting a futuristic museum in a metropolis on the moon). However, once the "injection" was given, the excellent guide (the authorized one) removed the needle from those leathery, docile bodies and sank into a silence that seemed to be awaiting the sound of God's trumpet.

Then the angel sang his song.

—RAINER MARIA RILKE

George Kordis, *Annunciation*, Private Collection.
Reproduced by courtesy of the artist.

I lingered carefully behind the altar, among the pitter-patter of those leaving. To make sure I was left alone and forgotten among those walls, I elevated, between me and every one else, a Hail Mary.

An angel appeared at once.

"I knew you would come at the Hail Mary. . . ."

"Our time will always be different from that of humanity. Human time is the *stipendium peccati* (the wage of sin): time was invented by men when they sinned; from that moment, the history of humanity had to be split into two: before and after Christ's redemption; and that gap became your time. You turned the world in a restless meridian that takes its shadow from the shaft of the cross. The less you humans sin, the more the voracious shadow of time fades away. Enter the cloister of a monastery and you'll see that time there is almost completely reabsorbed by eternity. Our clock is a circle without hour hands."

"Is this the great secret you came to reveal to me today? *But I could reveal to you another similarly ancient one: that you angels envy this earthly time of ours. Perhaps because you don't have a history wearying you down—perhaps. Yet, history is still amazing, don't you think? Wouldn't you angels have liked to experience a Roman Empire, or the Crusades, or that great moment when the bulging Venetian galleys patrolled the*

Mediterranean against the pirates? Wouldn't you like to have the 'Middle Ages,' my dear angel? . . . Your history instead has only one significant episode that occurred billions of centuries ago and now is fading away: that palace conspiracy, when the world was not yet born. And you don't even have children to whom you can tell (thus making it new again) about that one day when swords collided there in heaven, against Lucifer and his rebel army of angels. And so you keep aging thousands of years in an instant, like a noble gentleman with no heirs, the only surviving member of a very old family on which weighs a coat of arms given after some remote glorious feat, and of which he himself has only a vague recollection. Yet, he still remains the stubborn guardian of it, in a perpetual dusk, lodging in an old and forgotten castle.

"You have no memories. And your only hope, even if you don't confide it to anyone, is that the Lord will send you on one of those rare missions of yours on earth. (How sweet it is to return in the evening, from the valleys down here, with your wings a little dirty of human dust; and to rest on the clouds, finally a little tired; but then your pride prevents you from talking about it amongst you, lingering for too long on those hours even only with your memory).

"Hence (come on, confide it to me in one ear), you get bored there in the heavenly spheres above, don't you? . . . as we little

creatures would get bored in heaven, after the Last Judgment,
if we had no memory of our days on earth . . . you know . . . like
our first communion, with the long ride in a carriage next to
the driver; or that evening when my father had to leave at once
because our grandfather had passed away, and our mother,
taken by sadness, allowed us children, already quite grown-
up, to sleep with her in the big canopy bed; or when later,
as young adults, we found our freethinker friend slipping
out of the confessional of an anonymous church somewhere
in the suburbs. In short: this blissful life of ours, which is
a sweet engagement with God before the big wedding in
heaven, with all the joys, the trepidations, the anticipation
of a longed-for love. Yes, let me whisper it to you in one
ear: even the blessed there in heaven, at times, get bored,
especially if they did not nourish the secret hope that one
day out of eternity it would dawn upon the good Lord to
bring all back down again; yes, into the garden, to stretch out
their legs a little.

"You diligent spouses, perennial housewives of heaven, you
envy us our engagement with the Lord. But above all, my dear
angel: you envy us Jesus, and you know it well; he was not born
for you: he exists only for us, wretched human beings that we
are. He turns his back to you and all of heaven, to linger down
here and talk to us. . . .

"Perhaps, my dear angels, for all your nine choirs, for all the mass of your glowing glory, the First Person of the Trinity was enough, as your summit: the eternal, the most high God the Father, eternally there to contemplate.

"And perhaps Lucifer, who once was one of your own, when he whispered to Jesus in the desert: 'If you are the Son of God, throw yourself down; for it is written, "He will command his angels concerning you," and "On their hands they will bear you up, so that you will not dash your foot against a stone"' (Matthew 4:6), *perhaps he sensed that you would have really let him crash to the ground of the holy city. . . ."*

∼

All this that I have written (in italics) I did not say out loud, but I silently meditated upon it while my fingers were toying with the rosary beads. It was a pause that had the same duration and the same stream of when, at a fountain, we wait for the bottle to fill up—without being able to speed up the time required.

"I have just come to tell you that you are the usual, incorrigible, absent-minded chump," said the angel after that awkward pause, with a hint of resentment in his voice. "Think about it for a moment: did you not forget something after your confession this morning? . . ."

"My penance!"

"Precisely . . . and do you happen to remember what it was?"

"Well, not exactly. . . ."

"The Virgin Mary for sure would not mind for you to recite one rosary."

"Which mystery? . . ."

He shrugged and started to leave.

"Angel, before you go, tell me the truth about this legend of the House."

He folded his wings.

"It all happened in May. For you humans, who keep track of the years, it was the 1291th year of Christ's redemption. The Virgin Mary wasn't as joyful, as she usually is during the month dedicated to her. I kept gazing upon her. And then one day she asked me to approach her, and when I did, she asked me if I knew of all the terrible things that were happening in the Holy Land. I told her that I knew that the Muslim Arabs had conquered the whole region, and were tyrannizing and massacring the Christians: 'You, Gabriel, Michael, and Raphael will go together to Nazareth; then, you will take my house and bring it where I will tell you.'

"Thus, once again, we were sent down from heaven among humans. The black mountains of Judah were

"You,
Gabriel,
Michael,
and
Raphael
will go
together to
Nazareth...."

George Kordis, *The Archangel Michael,*
Private Collection. Reproduced by courtesy of the artist.

silent, as that night when we came down to awaken the shepherds. But this time we were flying carefully in order to not awake anyone, two ahead and two behind, like monks feeling somewhat sad. Palestine's sky was still the same, heavy and tight, so susceptible to our angelic shape, that our shadows passed through curved and augmented. The House appeared to us as if made of mother-of-pearl, even though that night was moonless. We seized its four corners and raised it out of the ground with a simple flutter of wings. Meanwhile, the comet appeared, pointing in the direction of the constellation of Ursa Major, tilted at an oblique angle to the West. The House was not heavy, and at a simple push it seemed to move on its own, and we felt more like four lackeys around a carriage; we were flying with our uplifted faces over the violets of the night, with the tense but poised expression of those carrying out a mission. Soon we were over the sea (we could tell by the smell of wild fruit fermenting, and the echo of invisible choirs), but we did not see it: it was the Mediterranean, full of sunken triremes. The House became rapidly heavier to the point that we could not keep hold of it any longer. We put it down on a stretch of land: and dawn broke soon after that. The land in question was called Trsat, and was in Croatia. With the first morning light, some local residents saw an exotic building located in a place where they had never seen, until then, neither house nor cabin. Soon they were all rushing around, cheering and admiring the mysterious building made of small red stones. And for just over three years and a half they lived revering the House, proud of that unexpected privilege. Then one day—it was Advent, the season when in heaven we are even more concerned of you humans—the Virgin Mary summoned us again, and said that she could not but dream of a new place for her House in the most beautiful garden in the world: in a land of oranges, white bullocks with crescent-shaped horns, songs of peasants intoned while returning from the fields; a country with a meek and firm faith.

"This time we had no need of the Comet to indicate our path. We left the people of Trsat with a bit of sadness, and glided with the House straight to Italy. Here, too, the Virgin Mary was not satisfied with the location of our first landing, and had us move her House again, but just a little (how human the Mother of God seemed to us at that moment, almost uncertain, or apprehensive!). Finally, the hills of the central Apennine pleased her: and her smile, sweetly triumphant, radiated over the precious home. It was 10 December 1294. After this transfer,

Gabriel, Michael, Raphael, and I rested seven days and seven nights."

I gave a look around:

"And is it still as it was then?"

"Nope; up to 1531 the House kept its original layout: one central entrance (which proves to the skeptics that it was really a house and not a shrine especially built on the site). And the altar was at the center of the long wall. Later, Pope Clement VII decided to create two new entrances in order to facilitate the ever more abundant influx of pilgrims. And the altar was also moved to the east side, thus allowing the faithful to pay homage even to the fireplace; see there how the soot turned it black; and there are still remains of the porridge prepared by the Virgin Mary; . . . The fireplace is another proof that this is an authentic house."

"But how did they manage to make changes to the miraculous abode?"

"In effect, the builders hesitated for a long time, and with good reason: for when the first worker chipped away at the sacred wall with his pickaxe he fell struck to the ground. Then they took courage, and the Virgin Mary no longer opposed the project. She also did not object when the unruly troops of the Directorate, led by Napoleon, pocketed the precious jewels adorning the statue made in her honor, and carried the statue itself all the way back to Paris."

"Was the statue ever returned?"

"Yes, it was; five years later, when the Consul gave it back to Pope Pius VII."

"Earlier you mentioned that there are some skeptics."

"More than skeptics, they are fierce detractors. The miracle of the House's relocation is one of the most fascinating ones, and more eloquent than a hundred *summae theologicae*; after the miracle was ascertained, many nonbelievers and Protestants have converted. Yet, it would be too naïve to think that there are no doubters who, armed with lack of faith and skepticism, are ready to deprive the miracle of its divine dignity while reducing it to an old wives' tale and raw material for bigotry. Hence, since the first book against the miracle of the Holy House of Loreto by the apostate Petrus Paulus Vergerius in the Renaissance, the waves of atheism and agnosticism have often been too keen on sweeping this island of rock emerging on a strip of the Italian land, a true miracle of a dawn in winter."

"And what evidence can you offer to strengthen the faith of the believers?"

"Well, I could bring to your attention a wall fresco, discovered in Gubbio, and officially dated in the first half of the thirteenth century. It depicts that mission of ours of transferring the House from Trsat to the territory of Recanati in the Italian Marche region, thus indicating that the truthful and miraculous account of the facts did not originate in a later era, when the origin of the building was lost in the mists of time, but was the same of today, already within a short time from the first appearance of the House. But, of course, even more convincing is the chemical analysis of the stone used to build the holy abode that incontrovertibly proves that it was not built in Loreto.

"And finally, I will bring up for you one of the many papal approvals that have been granted throughout history. It is a decree by Pope Benedict XV. At that time, the Holy Congregation of Rites asked—following an order of the same Congregation to suppress almost all local feasts on the liturgical calendar—to keep the feast of Loreto, declaring it the most important sanctuary of Christendom.

"The pope responded by proclaiming December 10 as a 'feast to be celebrated as a double major feast by all the dioceses in Italy and its islands.'

"But follow me," the angel said, taking my hand, "to see God's own pronouncement on the matter. We angels have even left an everlasting memorial to the Nazarene origin of the House, for all of St. Thomas the Doubter's most stubborn companions."

I followed him inquisitively. We approached the main door, and very close to it I noticed that several large slabs of stone on the floor of the shrine were dislodged. Driven by curiosity, I went closer, and what was my emotion when I saw myself at once on the brink of a precipice where the bricklayers had to descend. I knew from my readings that the top of the Loretan hill was accessible only by donkey, but I would have never imagined that the holy House rested on the edge of such a cliff! How could one claim that the holy House was built in the place it occupies, when its front door is there opening onto the void?

At night, alone in your holy dwelling, Lord, I had a consoling thought: more and more humans forget you (or live as if they have forgotten you), but keep counting the years since your first coming. For this humanity that ignores or denies you, each reference to the year is an act of worship, a prostration in front of you: two thousand years ago our own destiny was created, Christ was incarnated and became man. Perhaps no other profession of faith is left for us than that: the more automatic and smoothed out by convention and habit, the more conspicuous and enduring. From the hasty bookkeeper's key strokes on ledgers, to the certificates and licenses filed by office clerks, as well as headers and footers of dramatic love letters, this drop of your precious blood stands out unwaveringly and admonishingly like a tacitly eloquent blind prophet in his tunic, among a crowd of sinners and merchants.

Thank you, Lord, for conceiving this stratagem—this second Eucharist—so you are with us on every page, in every human interaction. And may this lasting profession of faith alone, save us.

THE
VISITATION

. . . the land flowing with milk and honey

—DEUTERONOMY 31:20

I COLORED MY ATLAS BY MYSELF. For each country, I mixed its most typical products on a palette and watercolored every little map with a unique vibrant color that corresponds to the exact tone we conjure up in our imagination when we close our eyes and think of that particular place.

To color France, for example, I created a blend of cosmetic products and the yellow straw color of champagne. For Alaska, I used ice cream and bearskins, and for the Republic of the Congo, a lion's maw and coconuts. Doubtless, it makes for a delightful circumnavigation of the world, suitable for a rather unadventurous daydreamer. Distances here can also be covered by using one's nose because each map, once colored, retains the flavor of the ingredients used, and an experienced explorer, with eyes shut and nose to the paper, can tell you without mistakes: this is Sri Lankan rubber, that is the Volga river caviar. . . .

I colored the Holy Land with a lot of milk, a few dates, and a honeycomb.

The Virgin Mary set off on a trip to this tiny little corner of the world—which I colored with a freshly-milked ivory tint—just south of Jerusalem where Saint Elizabeth lived: the hill of Ein Karim.

She usually did not go to the countryside, but that year she decided to kill two birds with one stone: inform her aunt of the future event, and rest a little now that she was expecting, which made her feel a tad fatigued.

Ein Karim was the ideal site. A kind of bucolic and sophisticated *Brianza*, all dark green mottled with sheep, cows, and in the barnyards the placid sight of the farm animals, like the little chicks picking at millet seeds.[1]

Saint Elizabeth was the epitome of the perfect aunt. She was not the aunt of the whole round world only because the inadequate means of communication in those days tied the majority to their turf. But no human being, king or publican, Roman soldier or leprous person whatsoever, would have ever thought of calling her anything but aunt. She was one of those women who come into the world to undertake the profession of the compassionate old maid, the loquacious neighbor from across the street, ever-present at every birth, wedding, or funeral, wholeheartedly industrious and pious. Almost certainly, she married Zechariah, the good priest, only by mistake. However, she immediately put her cards on the table and, in the blink of

1. Brianza is a geographical, historical, and cultural district of Northern Italy.

an eye, she *adopted* her husband, who became her favorite among the already many adopted nephews and nieces she had: old maid she felt, and old maid she wanted to die. Moreover, her barrenness confirmed to her and to the world that she was not born for the remarkable mission of mother and wife, but to take on the more concealed role of maid of all work, an eclectic task that made her the irreplaceable béchamel that holds together all the neighborhood's "casseroles": engagements, dressings of the dead, bridal trousseaus, sprained ankles, and so on.

It took Mary's arrival to restore serenity in the old couple's home.

Elizabeth was a heck of a woman, born without the gland that governs the production of bad mood. But the disgrace of her husband returning home mute, because he doubted an angel sent to bring him the good news of his upcoming fatherhood, was a bit too much to bear—to say nothing of the growing gossip among the faithful, who that day were left wondering at his delay in the sanctuary, only to realize later on that he was unable to utter a syllable to them. . . .

An angel is always right, gracious heavens! She reflected. But who wouldn't be flabbergasted at such an announcement. A child? After forty years of marriage? And now there he was, shut in as punishment, like an animal secretly ill, with his pensive and coruscating eyes, a sad old fogey. True, he had never been particularly talkative, no, dear old child, but always know-it-all and curious.

What's more, that late pregnancy embarrassed her somehow. In her modest benevolence toward everyone, Elizabeth showed an acquired coherence of personality, an art of being always the same, which was important to her. It was a slightly pretentious, and somewhat provincial, affectation, like when we all put on airs, which nevertheless helped her get by and show goodwill. Now instead, nature took hold of her olive-gray body, which she had jealously preserved in the slender hieraticity of a Byzantine icon figure, and deformed it. An old woman with the bump! Elizabeth shuddered and, instinctively, bent so that the dress did not stay taut on her abdomen, which was still very thin, and by doing so, no one noticed that her lowered face was blushing.

"But people will put the blame on you," said Aunt Elizabeth when Mary finished telling her about the Angel's annunciation. "After all, you're still Joseph's betrothed. . . ."

"Here am I, the servant of the Lord" (Luke 1:38), was the only answer Elizabeth found in Mary's eyes, which were slowly rising on her as the wings of the sun.

George Kordis, *Annunciation*, Private Collection.
Reproduced by courtesy of the artist.

"Crazy old woman that I am!" jumped Aunt Elizabeth, shaking off all the moldy hypochondria of those past days with a good giggle. "My son has to prepare the way to yours, and here I am setting a bad example to you." She squeezed Mary's shoulders affectionately, and this forced her to get up and follow her aunt into the kitchen.

"Let's make some candy brittle with honey, almonds, and raisins. One of my old-time specialties, what do you say, Zechariah? . . ."

The old man was rhythmically agitating the milk with a plunger in the churn.

"Do not be afraid, Zechariah, for your prayer has been heard. Your wife Elizabeth will bear you a son, and you will name him John."

"How will I know that this is so? For I am an old man, and my wife is getting on in years."

"I am Gabriel. I stand in the presence of God, and I have been sent to speak to you and to bring you this good news. But now, because you did not believe my words, which will be fulfilled in their time, you will become mute, unable to speak, until the day these things occur." (Luke 1:13–20)

Since the day God made him mute, that was all Zechariah kept on doing. And now their house was overflowing with milk and butter.

ὁ ἅΓιος   ΙῶΟ
                 ὁ ΠΡΟᾺΟξ

ὅΤᾺ ΟΙᾺ ΠᾺς
χοΥGΙΙΙ Ὁ θε
ΟΥ ΛΟGΟ ΟΙ ΙᾺΙ
GΙΙΙᾺΤΟΙΙ ᾺΙΙΟΙ
χΟΙ ΤΟΙΙ Ε°Ὰ
ᾺΥᾺΤᾺΟΟΙΙ.

George Kordis, *Saint John the Baptist*, Private Collection.
Reproduced by courtesy of the artist.

⚮

*L*ike two caravels on a placid sea, the pregnancies of the Virgin Mary and Elizabeth proceeded quietly and smoothly. By the end of September, both their bellies were tight as a drumhead and arched, precisely like two sails.

The silence surrounding them was increasingly intense and rustling, almost as if the world, in a secretive and respectful cooperation, pretended to be asleep in order to uncover the mystery. Someone, I am sure, was constantly lending the ears to hear the hidden blending of fluids and liquids that generate life: the life of a man and the life of God. But the secret could be unveiled only by looking at the countenance of the two mothers' faces: the maiden-mother, with her warm brown braid; and the elderly woman, whose pregnancy had restored in her an almost childlike smoothness of skin.

George Kordis, *The Archangel Gabriel*, Private Collection.
Reproduced by courtesy of the artist.

Fructus
ventris
tui. . . .

For all women, pregnancy is a completely new biological dimension. She who carries life within her falls asleep in the lethargic torpor of nine moons, even though for the rest of her family she puts up with a fabricated, dreamy wake. If only men would find out that *during that time* she *knows all there is to know*, they would assail her with annoying and unpleasant questions. The most eager and arrogant would torment her:

"Tell us what life is. . . ."

"Why then do we die? . . ."

"Do you give birth first to the soul, or to the body?"

All the way down to the most narrow-minded that would ask her to reveal where is the long-searched-for hidden treasure, or a good combination to win the lottery.

A pregnant woman walks on water. But the Lord, in his benevolent wisdom, does not let women speculate on this mysterious state of collaboration with the Creator of all beings. For that reason no woman, not even one habitually inclined to gossip, has ever revealed to any other the secrets that the Lord has unveiled to her during pregnancy. In effect, hardly ever was it granted to a pregnant woman to perform miracles.

~⌐

𝒪nce upon a time, a pious peasant of the Dauphine region (in Southeastern France), named Remy, joined the army of Raymond of Toulouse and went as a crusader to the Holy Land. He had left his wife pregnant, and made a vow to the Virgin Mary promising that his child will be consecrated to her. And then one night, under the walls of Ascalon, Remy was on the verge of dying from a stroke of spear. At that same moment, his wife awoke with a start, and immediately realized what was happening: "O Mother of God, come to my aid and help me!" The Virgin Mary at once appeared: "Do you want him back and safe? Go to him and . . ." (she whispered something in her ear).

And so the angels carried the bride through the air with her miraculous viaticum. Under the tall walls of Ascalon, almost touching the stars and dotted with agave, in the glittering of moonlight, the injured Remy had already lost a lot of blood and, exhausted, was lying in the most languishing agony. Silently, his wife curled up next to him, took in her hands his bleeding head and laid it on her belly, remaining in that position for three days and three nights. And then, at dawn on the fourth day, Remy awoke and rose straight up: he was healed. His wife got up as well. But miraculously her body had become smooth and virginal again: the life she had had within her had been transfused to revive Mary's devout crusader.

$\sim$

$\mathcal{D}$uring that year, the region of Ein Karim was flooding with milk. The miraculous conception of the Son of God had deeply exalted the fertility of the land as well, compelling it to produce, in great abundance, the first food for the still unborn child of God.

Thus, while the blood in Mary and Elizabeth's breasts was being distilled in milk, causing tissues, through a network of burning veins, to swell up, the surrounding land, diligently following the two women's lead, swelled a tide of milk, as if touched by Moses's rod.

Even the animals in the barns were struck by a strange epidemic, causing their udders to fill up with a speed and frequency that was tenfold the usual.

As soon as the phenomenon spread, not all the farmers were able to batten down the hatches in a timely fashion, and a few cows and goats, let out to pasture from dawn to sunset after the regular milking, were driven mad by their swollen udders, which started to swell up disproportionately within a few hours, and suddenly rushed down a gorge.

Then, that same night, at the light of a campfire, the people took counsel and ruled that the miracle had something to do with the young bride from Galilee. It was also decided that the cows, sheep, goats, and all other female animals that had recently brought forth life would not leave the barns.

Zechariah also had four animals, all females, and just ready to give birth. And since from the time of his mysterious speech mishap the poor priest had almost completely neglected his affairs, no one noticed the overflowing condition that afflicted the animals.

One evening the Virgin Mary went to the barn: she had an irresistible desire—one of those piercing, bizarre pregnancy cravings—for the intense smell of steamy litter, to feel the animals' pelts and skins, and their warm breaths, all combined with the feminine odor of hay in the dark.

At the end of a short aisle, seated, an angel was milking. Had someone else arrived he would have disappeared at once. Instead, the angel knew that it was the Mother of God and smiled, continuing to milk, in all his beauty, without a hint of sweat.

"Why, Gabriel?"

"These creatures are preparing their gift for your child. But they are too generous."

"I see. But you must return to the Lord. We'll hire someone. But now go, Gabriel."

"Fiat mihi secundum verbum tuum" (let it be with me according to your word; Luke 1:38). . . .

And I also, O Mary, replied in the same manner, when you sent to call me to come to Ein Karim to become the dairy boy for Zechariah's animals.

I went up to Ein Karim and there I learned what happiness is. Already climbing the slope of the mountain I had the feeling of lightening up, as if I were ascending the circles of Mount Purgatory, or as if a twister sucked me in an anticyclonic area of happiness. Behind me, the landscape scenery faded away, and as I proceeded, the colors of the flowers and everything else gleamed more vividly, closing in on a circle of horizon increasingly narrow but richer in pigmentation.

I felt as if I were in the Garden of Eden, and was overwhelmed by a most acute sense of expectation. I was certain that once I reached my destination my longing desire would be fully satisfied, and I would finally find happiness.

I was so galvanized by this insight that when I entered Zechariah's porch and saw the Virgin Mary seated on a wicker chair, I said:

"Does happiness live here? Give it to me!"

"I am waiting for the Messiah to come. Everyone here awaits his coming."

"So you also are *waiting* for something you don't have yet?"

"All human beings are never short of that which faith ensures and what hope anticipates."

"And are you happy?"

"The realm of expectation is the realm of joy, in every aspect of life, be it big or small. Touched to tears, for centuries prophets have been announcing his coming, and now the time of his birth has arrived. This is the most wonderful time in the history of humanity. The door is about to open on something utterly new, and our hearts are taut as bows. In three days, go through the cities: children are already happy and their hearts burn like roasted chestnuts; they speak about and dream of shimmering toys that they will keep smelling to get a good whiff of heaven, where they believe they have been made. But even happier are their parents. They come home from work late because they remain with their hands in their pockets steaming up with their breath the deli and toy store windows. They smile and feel good; and no longer curse the cold, because in just a few days they will more fully enjoy the blazing log in the fireplace. At home, with timid fingers, they decorate the Christmas tree and prepare the crib, forgetting the pain that they may have inflicted upon others, upon Jesus. . . .

"And then the Messiah will come and my sufferings will begin. The straw will scratch him. Herod will want him dead; Simeon will show me the seven swords of my sorrow. They will scourge him, crown him with thorns, and then crucify him. And children in rich comfortable homes will eventually crush with hammers their new toys."

Yet, from that day, I learned to be happy.

*"for centuries prophets
have been announcing
his coming. . . ."*

George Kordis, *The Prophet Elijah*, Private Collection.
Reproduced by courtesy of the artist.

George Kordis, *King David*, Private Collection.
Reproduced by courtesy of the artist.

George Kordis, *The Prophet Isaiah*, Private Collection.
Reproduced by courtesy of the artist.

She seeks wool and flax,
and works with willing hands.

—PROVERBS 31:13

∿

$\mathcal{I}$ always saw the Virgin Mary seated. I could not tell if she was tall or small. I would bring her a cup of milk, fresh from the cow, three times a day, at dawn, in the late afternoon, and before going to bed, when Aunt Elizabeth would poke a nice and warm ruby-colored fire in the fireplace, to dissolve in joy, with a little cooked must, the first chills of autumn. After all, I would spend the whole day milking those inexhaustible udders that reminded me of Jupiter's cornucopia, and my poor fingers were drunk with milk.

Zechariah's toil increased as well. The old man kept silently churning the milk occasionally splashing himself with cream, and would implore us with his big eyes; their eloquence was accentuated by the contrast between the ivory-colored cornea and the thick, tar-black eyebrows.

The time spent around the fireplace was the finest hour of the day. Aunt Elizabeth would fry her famous ravioli or stir the roasting chestnuts. I would remain standing in a corner, as a good servant, with my sleeves rolled up and arms at my sides a bit away from my body. When the Virgin Mary would tell me to sit with them, I would clean my red hands on my apron, more out of politeness than anything else, and I would sit next to the fire poker. We would then spend the time telling stories in turns. Zechariah would keep the time with his constant churning. And the Virgin Mary would begin. So little did she talk during the day that every night her voice seemed each time new. If there was one thing that the Virgin Mary loved above everything else, it was silence. In point of fact, she told us the following story.

"There once was a monk who lived in a monastery in Umbria who imposed upon himself, to more fully do penance and purify his soul, a vow of perpetual silence. His confreres would say that the venerable monk had not uttered a single word to anyone for seven years. One night a fire broke out in the convent; it was already consuming a wing of the cloister, and the chapel itself was in danger. The monks, all agitated, run to his cell and interrupt his prayers: 'Father, our convent is on fire!'

"The old man went out, and told them to lead him to the site of the blaze; he then stopped in front of the fire, and stretched out his arms, saying: 'Flames, die out!' At these words, matured after seven years of silence, the tongues of fire were tamed, and in a few seconds they were swallowed by the ground."

~⌒

"Once upon a time," continued Aunt Elizabeth while handing out another handful of roasted chestnuts, "there was a pirate, whose crimes were too many to count. This wicked man had once asked the Virgin in prayer not to die without a confession. Now it happened that on a day of a great storm his ship sank. And while his companions were all dead, he was left drifting on the furious waves. The fish, which had already gulped down the entire crew, chewed up his entire body, but left his head, which continued to bounce from wave to wave until a vessel full of friars, who were all on deck reciting devoutly the Rosary, passed by chance.

"'Hey, you on the vessel, in the name of the merciful love of Christ, the Son of Mary, who wants to hear the sins of a scoundrel like me? . . .'

"A moon ray was shining on that mask of pain, with his hair plastered on his forehead with saline water and his insane eyes. All the friars leaned over the bulwarks, put on their good old stole and yelled:

"'Go ahead; in the name of our Lord Jesus Christ we will listen to you.'

"The confession went on forever, not only because the pirate's sins were innumerable as the fish of the sea, but also because the storm was bucking the vessel all to the seventh heaven and then all the way down, with the good friars' heads deep into the abyss where the pirate's voice went lost. Finally, at dawn, the pirate recited the act of contrition so remorsefully and penitently that the storm was silenced, and the sea became calm as a sheet. As a result, the pirate died in peace at last."

It was my turn now. I also wanted to tell a story demonstrating my devotion to the Virgin Mary.

"A knight decided to go to a monastery to do penance, but the monk assigned to instruct him was unable to teach him anything, apart from the Hail Mary; there was nothing else he was able to say during the long hours of prayer. After his death, a plant sprouted on his tomb. On each leaf of that beautiful plant was written *Ave Maria* in golden letters. The astonished monks all came running and started to search for the roots of the plant. In the end, they were found clinging to the heart of the deceased knight."

It was time to go to bed. Only the agony of the last log was left on the andirons, and Zechariah, with his mute destiny of milk and butter.

~

*F*all was aging like a sweet thickened wine, almost made of mother-of-pearl, left to rest. I was able to notice the seasonal change from the growing number of dead leaves enriching the litter of my barn.

I have always believed that men live only in the fall, if to live means to jump off the seesaw of joys and sorrows, and finally find oneself in true silence. In fact, when you think about it, life in winter turns into a fierce defense against the hostilities of the season. Its cold mists take away from us the sky, and with it our perspective. Crouched in the trenches of our homes, it is a bit like a spell of military life.

Summer instead is a great celebration, but, as in all festivities, one is always slightly drunk, and we tend to sleep too much.

Spring makes us very negative. The equinoctial temperament whips our senses, and the pollen stupefies us. "It is spring," we say, "I must be happy. . . ." And instead we are in a bad mood. An unhealthy desire to procreate leaves us restless in our beds. And when no one is around to see us, we smash the buds on the trees.

In the fall, we come to know the exact and appeased feeling of our human destiny: the indifferent shortening of a shadow under the direct meridian light, until it disappears, just as the season. But we are not deprived of some merciful consolations, as the fallen leaves that become golden, and sweet musts are there to give us back our youth.

These were my thoughts during the day, while squeezing the cows' pendulous teats and rhythmically directing the resounding jets of milk on the inside copper of the bucket.

A sharp and healthy smell emanated from the animals, with their long and well-rounded backs. Had it taken a dusty consistency, I would have taken them, all haloed in their outlines, for holy animals.

I would then think of Zechariah. No doubt of course, women are far superior to men. It would have never occurred to a woman to doubt the words of an angel, even if the angel had said to her, "Do you not know that the world is square?" Zechariah instead, being the bighead that he is, started immediately to put the notion through the grinder of logic, "But if so and so, then can it really be . . . ?"

What a fool. No wonder the angel had knocked him down. Too bad for him. Dawn, noon, and sunset would pass by through the gangly little window in the barn with their three complexions: blonde, brown, and fawn.

I kept wondering why women were so superior to men. And one day, out of the blue, I finally understood. Everybody, men and women alike, was created by God; but only a woman was chosen to bear Christ, the Word of God made flesh. In other words, Mary bore God in her womb. We men, after all, know the Lord only by word of mouth.

The animals would strike their hooves on the stony ground to drive away the horse flies. Then, turning their heads backward with their exorbitant eyes, they would clank their chains. They had the eyes of Zechariah.

You are stately as a palm tree,
and your breasts are like its clusters.
—SONG OF SONGS, 7:7

$\sim$

$\mathcal{D}$uring that time, I personally experienced the extent to which women are superior to men. Just listen to what happened to me.

I would go almost every day to Jerusalem to sell the milk that we had in abundance. It was not all that easy to get there because of the weight of the full jars, and the return climb was hard as well. But soon that grueling job became for me the most pleasant of walks.

Her name was Miriam; she was sixteen years old, and her laughter was baffling like a roe deer hastily vanishing in the woods.

She lived on the outskirts of the city, precisely in that ambiguous area where you are no longer in the country-side, but neither have you reached the city center.

From the earliest visits, she allowed me in her big kitchen, where she would offer me refreshments and where we would spend a long time together, almost always alone. Her company was like a fountain, and I was a traveler bleeding at the hands of brigands, under the sun of the road to Jericho.

It did not take long for my absences from Ein Karim to stretch so much that when I was back to the barn my animals had been waiting for me for quite some time with impatient bellows, and I would find their udders taut as drums.

But the Virgin Mary would always wait for my return instead of taking some afternoon rest, to spare me the humiliation of sending others to milk the poor animals.

One day at noon, Miriam and I were in her wide kitchen. The flies were thick and heavy, as if presaging death. The windows were open, and Miriam was drying the dishes. She suddenly asked:

"Is it true that the woman of Galilee is a witch?"

"And why would you say that?"

"Well, because they say that she is the cause of this milk epidemic, and that she is pregnant of a calf's head. . . ."

I laughed, but did not offer any explanations.

"And yet," she insisted, "there is something strange about her pregnancy. Everybody says so. Come on, tell me!"

From the first day I arrived, the Virgin Mary had told me not to trust anybody that I knew. And the fear of breaking such a big promise was clearly showing on my face at Miriam's insistence, while simultaneously exasperating her curiosity. For sure, after that afternoon she changed toward me, which made me suffer very much; and a few tears dripped into the bucket while I was milking the animals.

Sustain me with raisins,
refresh me with apples;
for I am faint with love.

—SONG OF SONGS 2:5

❧

𝒥 did not see Miriam for a week as we were busy with the grape harvest: I had told her to expect me for the following Saturday.

Even grapes that year were well developed and extremely plentiful, and the Virgin Mary came with us to harvest the ones that hung at shoulder height.

The day I went down to Jerusalem I found Miriam's house deserted. I went in: the kitchen was gloomy and silent. When my pupils, which had been obscured by the glare outside, gave me my sight back I saw a tiny cot in a corner. I ran: Miriam had her hair softly loose, and her face was a lamp, with her eyes wide open. She kept silent while I kissed her hands and the sheet, mumbling questions. Finally she whispered that she was near death. Why? Because she loved me.

"My love, you have revealed the joys of heaven to me, and without you I can no longer live. So I feel that life is escaping me, and I rejoice."

"For heaven's sake, Miriam, I will never leave you, if that is what you want! We'll buy a small house in Ein Karim, and I'll milk cows all around the entire region. . . ."

"It's useless, my beloved, the witch, pregnant with the calf's head, has decreed our separation and death."

"My sweet girl; my foolish and silly girl! What you call the calf's head . . . is the Messiah of the people of Israel. . . ."

All at once, like a gush, out came a baffling laugh from that pile of tatters and braided hair, like the flight of a deer in the woods. And after that, Miriam ran down the stairs in her shirt, knocking over a wicker basket full of linen.

"Ah! I knew I was right. . . . What a funny thing: the Messiah is a calf! A calf!"

⁓

" . . . *Forgive us our sins, now and at the hour of our death.* Amen."

When I had finished my fiftieth Hail Mary on my rosary, the Virgin Mary made me even say a *Salve Regina* as penance for smashing the pitchers in anger before returning from Jerusalem.

"And now you are forgiven. Go and learn not to trust women all the time—and the same goes for men."

At that point, Elizabeth came in with her hands to the sky, shouting that Zechariah, gone mad, had plunged his head in the milk churn, perhaps with the unconscious instinct to take his own life.

But that entire day had ended with a dash of humor. Laughing, we dried the old man's innocent face and beard all drenched in milk.

At what price God gives his kingdom
and eternal life!
God may grant both to a penitent,
for a single prostration.

—ANGELUS SILESIUS

But that night was not a quiet one for the Virgin Mary. I was the only one to notice it, as I saw the light filtering through her room at an unusual hour, and drawing a little bit closer, on tiptoes, I caught the following agitated bickering.

SATAN: "Once again, you have taken my own gain by force!" (*To himself*) "Just when I think I landed a soul, this little woman comes along and steals the juicy meatball from my plate. She will never leave me in peace: this one woman is running me out of business. Damn me if this is not being fooled!"

VIRGIN MARY: "You are completely wrong. If I take away from you the man who has turned away from God, according to justice I do not take from you anything more than what belongs to God. I am not swindling you, traitor that you are, if I call a sinner to repentance."

SATAN: "(*Secretly nostalgic*) And yet, after all, shouldn't I be deserving of some compassion too? Haven't I lost heaven's infinite bliss, after all? I too am a creature of

God, and you should have some respect for me as well. For one sin only I was cursed forever; whereas humans, even if they sinned a thousand times, would always be forgiven. You give them hope, all your care is for them, and so you tear them away from my clutches, by force, just when they are cooked to perfection.

"And (*cunning and rational*) do you know what else? You should reflect on the fact that the sinners of the world will hurt you a lot more than I will: at their hands, not mine, your son will be killed!"

VIRGIN MARY: "Go away! Get out, you serpent of old! Your sin was so heinous and great that it cannot find forgiveness: nobody forced you to sin, but only your pride caused you to offend God; and what is worse, you always persisted in offending him. Whereas sinners are subject to a thousand temptations, to say nothing of your snares; they are exposed to many dangers, and it is only right that they are forgiven through repentance. You instead have always been the proudest being of the entire creation, a criminal and a traitor, and it is only befitting that your damnation goes from bad to worse."

SATAN: "Right you are. But if I did not have Adam eat the apple your much-beloved sinners would not even exist, nor would Christ be conceived by you to come and save them."

VIRGIN MARY: "So, according to you, I should do like that judge, who released all the detainees from prison because, when you think about it, it was only for the sake of their wrongdoing that he earned his salary. . . ."

SATAN: "(*Humiliated*) Almighty God could have well created me so holy and pure that I would have never sinned. And today I would be in the good company of angels, where living is so sweet. What was his problem with that? What harm could have come to him from doing so?"

VIRGIN MARY: "But God *did* make you beautiful and good like the other angels; God also gave you free will so that you could choose for yourself, as they have done, between good and evil, and you alone have sinned: how could there be eternal glory if one, having the choice to do good, does not also have the choice to do evil?"

SATAN: "True, God gave me free will, but knew well that I would eventually sin, and so should not have created me. No, damn it, he should not have created me. Come on, give birth; soon we will have fun staring at your Christ hanging from the cross with his beloved flock making a dash for it—or dancing around in merriment. . . ." (*Then, growling, he disappeared. The Virgin Mary, exhausted, with this pain in her heart, fell to her knees before the crucifix and wept softly until dawn.*)

George Kordis, *The Crucifixion*, Private Collection.
Reproduced by courtesy of the artist.

THE
NATIVITY

Beth-lehem: House of bread

THE GUESTS BEGAN TO ARRIVE with the first shadows of evening. With their backs bent and their steps that made you think of people chilled to their bones, they were traveling, with their noses in the air, through the endless plains in twilight. The smaller children were pulling wheel toys with long strings, insignificant anticipations of the presents that they were expecting that night. Each person was unaccompanied and silent. And so were the families, proceeding without taking each other's arm, in small groups. The influx was concentric, and yet, the huge crowd, so silent and numb, seemed far less numerous. They all carried one or more packages well wrapped in pretty brown paper with golden ribbons, with the trademark labels of the most refined bakeries and brasseries, and would go quickly to place their gifts in the mouth of an already overflowing cornucopia. This immense, fluorescent cornucopia had its back to the sky and the tip of its horn was fused to a star, so as to form its tail.

All those men and women, even though they were of different eras and dressed in the most varied styles, seemed all seized by a similar concern. Their faces lightened up only when they would find on the table a card with their name as guests written upon it, and could finally stretch out their legs under a huge horseshoe-shaped table set. The influx of guests went on for several hours, because darkness had long fallen but still not all the seats were occupied. Those who came first, without giving signs of impatience, rarely spoke but preferred to pass the time filling up on bread, which they would pull starting from the crisper corners. And some, pulling a bit of bread here and a bit there, gobbled up so much of it that they had to be taken away in arms for gastric congestion.

Finally, when the clock stroke midnight, all the guests were in place. A fluttering of wings in the velvety sky was heard, and a flight of white angels soared above becoming a legion of waiters. But there was a first moment of confusion during which the service was at risk: a crew of bagpipers appeared simultaneously with the angels claiming that they were the only ones entitled to serve at the tables. After a brief altercation, during which the angels fluttered around terribly angry and the bagpipers kept smacking their foreheads and chins in the attempt to persuade their rivals, it was decided that the shepherds would play the bagpipes, the horns, and the drums, to entertain the gathering.

Then, and only then, did it become possible for the angels to begin to serve.

> *Dinner time is the most wonderful*
> *moment of the day;*
> *perhaps its purpose and*
> *flower.*
>
> —NOVALIS

*P*iglets, partridges, ducks, golden herons with fire in their beaks, boars with bird pies, creamy white sauce with sweet eggplant seeds in green sauce and Corsican wine, sausages, gelatin in silver bowls, golden meat pies, cups of silvery lemons in syrup, cherries in mugs with wine of Tyre, pink trout and golden pheasants, warblers, melons, fish salad, hedgehogs, frogs, stewed woodcocks, fricassee of pigeons, quails à la Mirepoix, lamb chops à la Bellevue, kidney pies, mushroom puddings, puddings with pistachios, pies of sea spider crabs, juicy and crunchy chestnut-colored roasts, salty beef marinated in light beer of Hamburg, Bavarian hare with wine from the Rhine region, wild goose à la Mecklenburg stuffed with apples and grapes with red cabbage, broiled thrushes, sausages with sauerkraut, caviar, smoked and salted fish, shrimps, fondue, polenta with little birds, spaghetti with clam sauce, pasta with fresh tomato sauce . . .

. . . and on top of it all an incessant shower of truffles . . .

. . . all overlooked by dark ruddy lobsters, Chinese monsters defending with their terrible pincer-shaped claws the most alabastrine, the most tender and delicious meat a gourmet could ever wish for.

But the cornucopia kept regurgitating. And the more the guests' bellies were filled (because to go on with the communal meal became less and less a true need of the body, and more and more a careful bet with one's palate) the more the frequency rate at which the cornucopia dished out the food seemed to the guests, due to a frightened psychic impression, increasingly accelerating. And not after long to the gourmet amateurs, who were already overwhelmed and gasping for breath, its mouth seemed the crater of a terrifying volcano that was frenetically burying its victims under lapilli of crustacean remains, and lava of oily mayonnaise.

At times it would happen that some gravy or a spurt of wine would end on the wings or robes of one of the angels. Instinctively, the clumsy diner would try to wipe away the stain with a napkin, but nobody ever found, upon that candid white, the disgraceful trace, or the exact point where it ended.

But the energies that by now had left the profane group of would-be food connoisseurs, already resting unresponsive, or dozing off, with their arms on the armrests, had found new outlets in a small wing of diners who, like disaster relief helpers, seemed to have found, amid the devastation, an inner strength.

A man in his fifties, all wrapped up in his hooded robe, had created his own little hermitage in a corner of the table, and isolated from all, with his feet on the table, was trying—clearly prevented from swallowing anything more through his mouth—to stuff down a turkey leg through his nostrils, while belching improperly. Of course, it was Monsignor Giovanni Della Casa, the author of the famous *Galateo*.

At another end of the table, four gentlemen—two in robes and two in gowns—were guzzling and joking affably, flaunting their unperturbed physical and mental condition. They were the renowned gourmets Marcus Gavius Apicius, Emperor Vitellius, Ciacco dell'Anguillara, and Bonaggiunta Orbicciani. This last one was giving a speech and telling the following story:

Long time ago there was in Lucca a notary whose name was Giannotto. His greatest delight was in the pleasures of the belly and the palate, and he used to say that men were born for nothing else but to eat one's fill from morning to evening. He also used to say that, after his death, he wanted to be stitched into the belly of a pig; nothing else was allowed to be used for his tomb. "I'm only doing what is fair," he would add, "since I have concealed so many of them in my belly, at least for once a pig can bury me in his."

Now it happened that Giannotto came to die, and even in his will was found expressed this desire of his, which many believed to be just a joke, good to tell at banquets; whereas the notary, who was rather corpulent, went so far as to indicate the enormous sow of his sty that he had chosen for his tomb. And so what he ordered was done. Once the sow was found, killed, and dissected, the notary was stuffed inside after which the sow was appropriately stitched back together.

But as the tale goes, by a trick of Beelzebub, as soon as Giannotto was put in the tomb of his choice, the sow came back to life, and at once she quickly took flight in the direction of the countryside,

chased in vain by the priest who still had to bless
Giannotto's burial site. Hence, it is believed that
somewhere around the world there is still a pig who
knows Latin and the law, and speaks with the voice
and authority of a notary.

The Magi from the East arrived by the time the moon
lit up that carnage of looted food and sleeping bodies. With
their inert heads and arms on the table, even the guests
seemed nothing more than recently caught game thrown
there by the hairy hand of a hunter. Necks of damselfish
and pink gills of trout were weaving secret romances under
the insidious light of the chandeliers.

The Magi did not decide to go in one direction nor in
another. They unloaded their goods from the camels and
dromedaries that kept whipping their sides with their tails.
They bowed primly in direction of the four cardinal points,
and all three, with their good crowns on their heads, sat at
table: Caspar all ivory, Melchior all saffron, and Balthasar
all ink.

They signaled the angels to go on and serve their
oriental spices. They had come from the Far East to sit
at table and dine. Behind each of them, an angel was
incensing with a golden thurible, a thurible of incense,
and a thurible of myrrh.

✧

The three were at the head of the table, at the midpoint of the horseshoe, speaking with their heads together, like thieves in a tavern.

"Do you know who is Jesus Christ?" wondered the one with the face of a crow, the only one who had not touched food the entire evening. And you could tell from the way he said it, that it was an obsession of his.

The bald man in a tunic, with the bored and haughty attitude of the ancient Roman at the height of imperial glory, sharpening his nostrils between thumb and index finger, replied that he vaguely remembered such a character of many years ago; but he also added that his memory could only associate him with a confusing number of opinions and events.

Herod, wearing a turban of the same color as his beard, burst out with a pasty and drunken voice:

"Gosh, sure I know: Jesus Christ is a man who came in the world to let us have a big feast at Christmas. Were we not to celebrate his birth, how could humanity justify such a solemn and collective food extravaganza? This is why Christ is called, if I remember correctly, the redeemer of the world."

"Do you know who is Jesus Christ?" repeated Judas with a paranoid voice. Then he added in a voice as low and menacing as the bogeyman: "Jesus Christ is at your back! He is *always* at your back. . . ."

Herod and Pilate turned abruptly in their chairs, with a wriggle of their backside typical of those who are told: "Look, there is an insect sliding down the neckline of your shirt!"

～

I forgot, in the midst of so many things to tell you, that on the plain outside there was also a thatched hut, and within, a manger with Baby Jesus, Mary, and St. Joseph. The thatched hut was burning but not consumed by the flames, and the very lengthy fire, like the beard of a prophet, ascended to the stars. I believe that nobody noticed the hut, because although it was situated in front of the opening of the horseshoe table, the guests were seated only along one side of the table; and thus, with their backs to that scene (time and again unnoticed anyway).

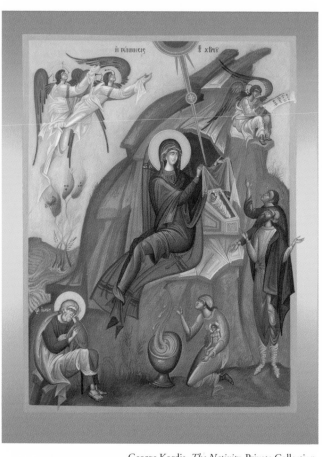

ἡ γέννησις τοῦ Χριστοῦ

George Kordis, *The Nativity*, Private Collection.
Reproduced by courtesy of the artist.

～

The three instead kept staring: Pilate and Herod were surprised, while Judas was hallucinating. The images of the Child Jesus in the manger that were passing on the retina of Herod's cloudy and bovine eyes, were that of a bottle amid the straw of the packing case. But wait, his tiny naked body did not look like a bottle after all. It was more like something between a worm, a bar of butter, and the cotton candy of the county fairs. He almost felt like he had to try that piece of meat with a fork two, three, four times.

He was so completely transfixed for a moment, while the sacrilegious thought invaded the watertight compartments of his spongy brain:

"Barabbas!" he yelled.

A heavy and gloomy man, with an unkempt beard, and all dressed in a black garment that was short enough to leave his legs and one shoulder bare, rushed jumping on the table. He was laughing, with wine-shot eyes, while overturning several glasses of wine with his unsteady feet; in one instance, the wine ended up on the white shirt of a lonely man who was smoking too many cigarettes, and who later decided to take his leave.

"No! I don't want you to come here, I want HIM . . ." pointing at the Divine Infant with his crooked finger. "I want to gobble him up! I am hungry again. . . . I want to scarf him down!"

"Do you know who is Jesus Christ?" asked once again Judas, as though talking to himself, with almost no voice.

Pilate kept looking at his beautiful hands. Then a fist slammed on the table: it was Herod's. All the glasses were shattered. The frightened angels flew away in flocks.

All the guests, men and women alike, woke with a start, but did not flee immediately because they noticed that there was still food on the table. They began to chew frantically. A second fist of Herod was heard:

"I want children's flesh!"

At this, the mothers, who had with them their little toddlers, were the most swift to disappear with the little ones under their cloaks like stolen books.

~

Then, everybody else, noticing that Herod's eye pupils were menacingly spreading like an evil bubble ready to burst and inundate the entire world, arose at once and, as fast as their legs allowed, disappeared, wandering into the night without saying goodbye to anybody.

George Kordis, *The Last Supper*, Private Collection.
Reproduced by courtesy of the artist.

I should not have been there that night in Bethlehem. After what happened with Miriam, the Virgin Mary had told me not to go to the Christmas dinner, adding that I would still be able to see the Child Jesus when they would take him to the Temple. And I, as it often happened, could not stay away from getting into trouble again, this time even more so: in fact, I did go in the end. However, to avoid being recognized, I dressed up as a Roman legionary. I will not tell you how uncomfortable I was with the breast-plate, like a snail in a shell that is not its own. And then there was that spear that I had to keep in my hand, whereas I would have so eagerly thrown it away in the first corner. But I had to keep up my disguise. I felt like one of those newly hired extras who, in a major crowd scene, think that they are the center of all the attention, and every gesture becomes heavier than a sack of potatoes. How were the Romans able to conquer the world all geared up like that?

But when I caught sight of Herod's beastly intentions, I truly felt like a legionary myself: it was necessary to save the child. The Virgin Mary and St. Joseph did not notice anything, captivated as they were in worshiping the divine infant; even the night wind could no longer stir their hair, or their clothes. I moved toward them. It does not matter any more if she recognizes me, I thought; I will go to hell all right, but at least the Child Jesus will be safe. The ear of Joseph was near:

"Get up! And take the child and his mother and flee into Egypt, and remain there until I tell you; for Herod is about to search for the child, to destroy him" (Matthew 2:13).

We had just disappeared into the freezing darkness of the night that already began turning into dusk, when Herod succeeded, with extraordinary efforts, to stand up. He was drooling all over, and a bulging vein of his forehead was pounding in his temple like a dying viper:

"Quit it!" he yelled. And threw the chair at the mouth of the cornucopia, from which the abundance of Christmas continued to regurgitate. Just then, a basket of eggs was coming out of the cornucopia that immediately became a giant, sizzling omelet.

And that turned out to be the only "massacre of the innocents" of the night.

Like all those men, who even when they commit the most horrible acts need to feel in the safety of a warm alliance with those of their kind, Herod shook with a sort of affection the arms of Pilate and of Judas:

"You will help me get revenge, won't you? . . ."

Pilate looked at his beautiful hands, and silently drew closer to a finger bowl in which he dipped his fingers still smelling of pecorino cheese.

Judah's eyes lighted up with a mirage involving blood, gold, and a noose:

"You do not know who is Jesus Christ. . . ."

When they also finally took leave, the shepherds, who had taken refuge under the table during Herod's outburst, popped out, with their unsophisticated rural faces and slippers tied up with straps from their ankles to their knees, improvising a feast with the leftovers of all those gentlefolks.

And from the comet continued to drop down, through the mouth of the cornucopia, turkeys, lobsters, and liqueur.

Were Christ born in Bethlehem a thousand times,
but not in you, you are eternally lost.

—ANGELUS SILESIUS

Tempus erat quo prima quies
mortalibus aegris incipit
et dono divum gratissima serpit.

(It was the time when the rest first
begins for weary mortals and,
as a gift of the gods,
most pleasingly creeps over them.)

—VIRGIL

I awoke with a start: three knocks at the door.

(Sleep had made a nest in the nape of my neck while I was in prayer, as I decided to wait until midnight on the kneeler. The Christmas tree was still visible by the light of a last red candle-end, all tears. I was dead tired after a long day spent in toy shops.

What a light in those stores: the toys were radiating all that white and warm light.

Under my shoe-soles there was a comfortable spongy carpet all over the floor. Please, I would also like to give it a look."

The clean-shaven salesclerk, winding up the little car that makes the curves by itself along the edges of the table, with an absent and cordial expression kept an eye out to ensure that nobody would touch anything. How many times did that clean-shaven salesclerk rewind it?

There were old ladies, hasty and demanding, with high black boots, sniffing toys as if they were truffles, not lending their ears to the lures of the clerk and pulling away tediously without buying anything, yet their arms were laden with packages, and I kept thinking what kind of superfine goods had been able to persuade those tough ladies to buy them: "Like this, you aim with the torpedo which is there, then the cartridge explodes, the spring snaps and smashes into pieces the battleship . . . then you reassemble it, like this."

. . .

Doll's saucers as big as pennies, with sausages and asparagus, and an egg that seemed it had seen a true plate only at a distance: the children for sure are not enjoying themselves there; they are like businessmen in the atrium of the stock-market exchange.

And the grown-ups? A little old lady with silver hair all dressed in black who is rubbing repetitively her hands, and constantly repeating: "Oh my goodness." . . . A mother next to an unattended table who will end up buying that doll which she examined last, under a pile of identical ones. A man with a cigar and a large fur coat who comes in and buys almost the entire store.

Everyone has a little guardian angel, mad with joy flying around their heads like an insistent bumblebee, and at times they shush it away with one of their gloved hands. All have at heart a *menu* meditated for a full year, and at their wrists a watch stuck on midnight—when, all of a sudden, they start out again on the freezing-cold road, with bubbles of vapor puffing out from their mouths. . . .)

George Kordis, *Gethsemane*, Private Collection.
Reproduced by courtesy of the artist.

"So, could you not stay awake with me one hour?"

—MATTHEW 26:40

~

*M*y limbs ached all over from the deep sleep when I got up to open the door.

St. Joseph's head was bald and frosted with fresh snow-flakes. The Virgin Mary was holding a bundle under her blue cloak, and for last, a Roman soldier, as soon as he entered, embraced me and then disappeared:

"Who was that?" I asked, yawning.

"It was you," said the Virgin Mary.

"Me?"

"Yes, your other 'self.' The mischievous one, the one who disobeyed my command not to come to Bethlehem tonight. Your good self instead has obediently stayed home, with the intention of waiting the child's birth in prayer; but I see that you are falling asleep."

"And where is the Roman legionary now?"

"He is now returned to you; the split is over."

"What was he doing with you?"

"He saved us. Joseph and I were absorbed in adoration, and Herod was about to kill the child. You have warned us on time, and made us flee."

"Did I? Then my wicked and disobedient self offered the greatest service to the Lord and humanity. . . . Had I not disobeyed you, we would be in deep trouble. Meanwhile, my good self was unable to finish the rosary without falling asleep. . . ."

"That's how it is at times," whispered the Virgin Mary; and she sat close to the fire.

"So, was he born?" I asked.

"Here he is," said the Virgin Mary, opening up her mantle.

George Kordis, *Mary and the Child Jesus*, Private Collection.
Reproduced by courtesy of the artist.

Adeste, fideles. . . .

⌒

I lay down on the floor. From that level, the house had a different scent. The polished wooden floor, the electrical outlets just above the baseboard of the walls, the wool cloths under the furniture; everything had kept its typical strong odor, almost of a domestic mushroom bed: the mushrooms of childhood. Childhood is a perpetual hunt for mushrooms, better still, a perpetual smell of mushrooms. Even the fresh and balsamic smell of the Christmas tree evaporated, leaving in its place, around my temples and coming from the bottom of the most derelict drawers of the house, that wonderful smell of mushrooms.

My mother entered. She was wearing her soft lilac satin apron, which she used to wear around the house twenty years ago, when she still kept her hair long, and used to make "a quiff" with hairpins in front of the dressing room mirror. I perched on her knees, looking instantly at the flower pattern of her apron in order to spot faces of monsters that my imaginative eye would promptly guess among all those flowers, so I could then hide, with a blissful thrill, my head in her bosom.

My father was drinking his tea with long sips, and with the chair a bit away from the table. He would then ask if I wanted to spell from the newspaper, and when I would read the newspaper title he would give me ten cents. From the kitchen came the clatter of the dishes that our maid was washing and the flow of water from the faucet. Outside, the cats would howl. It was that time of day when women and the house itself were the only ones in charge. They tacitly understood each other, and I am sure that if my father or I decided to go down the dark living room or bedroom to do something unexpected or unusual, one of the trinkets, no doubt a sentinel in disguise, would give the signal to my mother.

I was a strange child; before falling asleep in my white crib bed, I would ask Jesus "to send me the flu," so I could feel my mother's fresh hand on my feverish forehead.

The Virgin Mary's gift continued: the house smelt ever more of mushrooms, and I kept growing increasingly tiny, while my father became more and more young and skinny—just like when he was a boy.

Then my mind became confused, and I could only see the things close to me, which were very large, but I could barely make any sense of it all.

When the Virgin Mary saw that I had become the same size of her own child, she picked me up in her lap as well. She was wearing a satin apron with lilac flowers. With a sigh, she pulled out two breasts fresh as dew, and gave to the King of angels and me our Christmas lunch.

(Perhaps, you may wonder, as I did afterward, whether the Virgin Mary offered that divine gift to the disobedient Roman legionary, or to the sleepy devout child. The fact is, the Virgin Mary never thinks too much before granting a favor).

Outside, the cold ran naked through the streets, in all its youth, with black-fringed hair on the forehead, whipping all the passersby and dancing with broad gestures, and with liberated raised arms.

ΜΡ ΘΥ

ℹ️C ΧC

George Kordis, *Mary and the Child Jesus*, Private Collection.
Reproduced by courtesy of the artist.

THE
PRESENTATION

The monumental art,
the statues and the tombs,
the precious mosaics ... and the incense,
still fully act in response
to that need of deep and reassuring
stillness that our times
have aroused in us all.
—ANTONIO BALDINI

IF SOMEONE WOULD STOP ME, in head-on fashion, and ask me point-blank what is the thing I like the most, I think I would answer: the sun filtering through the stained glass windows of a church. We worry so much about what heaven is going to be like, and instead we can see it all along: in mid-air, pierced by the sunlight, all made of beautifully warm, watery colors.

I have spent entire days in my favorite cathedral, in Milan, enjoying the sun's retelling of the same biblical fact in three or four different tonalities, from dawn to dusk.

But I have always been a peripatetic pilgrim, and the churches of Rome are always more than just churches: they are cathedrals of the spirit.

All of them: from the basilicas of San Pietro and San Marco to the churches of Santa Maria in Aracoeli and Santissima Trinita' dei Monti; from the basilicas of Santa Maria Maggiore and San Giovanni in Laterano, to the little churches of San Saba and San Bonaventura on the Palatine; from the church of Santa Maria sopra Minerva (oh, the angelic windows of the Minerva . . .), to the one of the Gesù (my dear aristocratic and incomparable Gesù: *Ad majorem Dei gloriam . . .*).

When you walk in a church in Rome, you feel all the blood of the martyrs, which flows in a warm perennial river underneath the city, showering you like waves crashing against a cliff, and roaring back at you "Christ, Christ, Christ." Devotion here is in the same air you breathe, and you can almost touch it while a perpetual Lenten sermon makes its way through the air, leaving not a single freethinker standing as everybody falls to their knees. And all this terrible and venerable history piling up in ruins around you—crazy Caesars, fearful or frantic idols: nothing but a pile of rubbish waiting for a Cross to be planted there so that you, churches of Rome, with your breadth reproducing the archetypal breath of God, unaware of the past and the future, and alive only in the spirit of the present, which traverses the thick-padded quilt of your doorsteps to discover the large circles and the liturgical silences of creation.

Our fate has always been set under the arches of a cathedral. The church where Dante met Beatrice; Santa Chiara in Avignon, where Petrarch fell in love with Laura; and San Lorenzo in Naples, where Boccaccio met Fiammetta—these are milestones in our history: three poets fall in love, three worlds blossom. In the two churches in Paris of Saint Roch and Notre Dame, Manzoni and Claudel found, each in his own spontaneity, that faith which would give rise to monuments of progress.

Therefore, every well-bred person entering this extra-territorial area, where the foundations cling to heaven and where the murderer, embracing the altar, finds salvation and immunity against human justice, will find what he or she looks for—along with what they did not know they were looking for.

Hence, from early childhood I decided to spend the rest of my life in a church. But I did not want to become a priest: with my wobbly contralto voice, I served in the choir until I was fourteen; there were a bunch of us—white surplices and outstretched mouths—under a tawny-bony choirmaster who used to conduct with a pained expression on his face; it was ecstasy.

Together with the aforementioned stained-glass windows filtering the sunlight, the other great thing about life is singing. But singing in a church, blithely sailing with your voice over the roaring whirlpools coming from the organ, understanding just a word here and there of Latin like someone collecting shells under the first waves reaching the shore, is a blessing like no other.

And then I became tenor; and now that I am pretty old, I can still muddle through, with my vocal range encompassing the lower notes, as a hoarse baritone.

In short, I have always been in a church.

I did not want to become a priest. Because to study— my mother, who was a country teacher, always lectured me—means to turn away from what we already know, that everyone knows, "bread, home, and God," and set off on a long journey: you think you are arriving at distant places, perhaps reaching the sun there on the horizon, and instead, since the world is round, you go all around it, and then, there you are again, back to the starting point: "bread, home, and God." Only that now your hair has turned white.

Our ruin, my mother always used to say, is that the world is round. If it were a straight road, the one with longer legs would go further ahead. Instead, everybody has to come to terms with the same old things: "bread, home, and God." She was also convinced that before Adam's sin the world was straight and smooth as a tablecloth; but after Adam fell, God, in a fit of rage, bent it over his knee.

I did not want to become a priest. But to be sacristan is a completely different story. The sacristy is the antechamber of heaven, my mother often used to say. And I have always felt at home there: vestments, copes, reredoses, censers, ciboria, stoles, extinguishers; all things that taste of old, of dead people, of the souls in Purgatory. I keep them all in great order in their drawers, and kiss them because I know that if all of a sudden the end of the world arrives and the world plunges back into nothingness, they would still be there, everything in its place, by the will of God.

Besides, I like to be alone in church when everybody else—even that ghost of an octogenarian with her rosary—is gone. Then, I will idly, but carefully, sweep the pavement where beautiful tombs spread out: some of the carved bas-relief iconic portraits of the person buried in the tomb have been worn down by the incessant trampling of the faithful, and their flat, comical faces look like rabbits. It is then that I want—I have always wanted—to see the Lord. True, God *is always* with me, as the priest says all the time: God is there, in that white Host. Yet, why can God not

Η ΥΠΑΠΑΝΤΗ

George Kordis, *The Presentation*, Private Collection.
Reproduced by courtesy of the artist.

take a little stroll in his own house all dressed in red? After that, I make believe that I am sweeping, and from time to time I suddenly turn around.

"Lord, do not let your old servant see death without seeing you at least once!" That is why, after Christmas, I approach and lift the veil from every baby's face when they bring them to be baptized; you never know, it might be him.

This year, right on the first of January, a strange woman comes into church, all agitated:

"I want to baptize my child," she says to me almost in a threatening tone while I am pouring the blessed water in the stoup.

"The parish priest is out, there is no one at this time, come back in an hour."

"I need one now!" she answers back, almost screaming and grabbing my arm.

I shush her, but then I realize that there is something distressingly legitimate in her and her baby all bundled up. She drags me in a corner and, removing her shawl, she shows me the baby:

"He's dead . . ." she murmurs.

"Dead? But then you cannot. . . ."

Have you ever seen the eyes of a doe mortally wounded?

I shake my head and look around; then I walk to the baptismal font. Father Joseph won't see me, no one will ever know. . . .

"*. . . In nomine Patris et Filii et Spiritus Sancti*"
"*I am the Resurrection and the Life. . . .*"

The motionless little thing suddenly begins to jerk, a whimper . . . now he starts squealing.

We look at each other. The mother is ecstatic and kisses him, but does not look in the least surprised: this is precisely what she expected (women are not one bit surprised by a miracle).

I lift the pitiful shawl and study the face of that tiny creature, his blonde hair a golden halo upon his head.

Master, now you are dismissing your servant in peace, according to your word; for my eyes have seen your salvation, which you have prepared in the presence of all peoples, a light for revelation to the Gentiles and for glory to your people Israel. (Luke 2: 29–32)

But let us hope that Father Joseph never finds out.

THE FINDING OF
JESUS AT THE TEMPLE

Joy, which was the small publicity of the pagan,
is the gigantic secret of the Christian.

—G. K. CHESTERTON

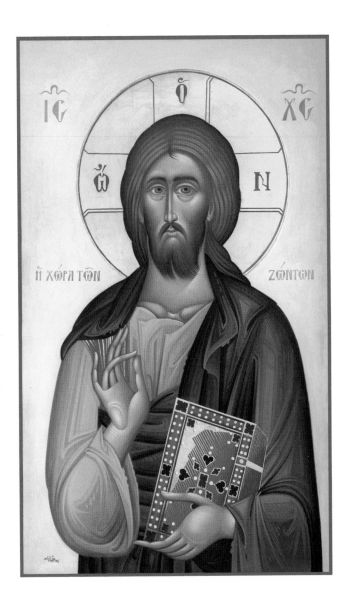

Feast of St. Aloysius Gonzaga—Summer solstice

 EAR OLD COLLEGE REFECTORY . . . my childhood made its nest in your corners. There you are, still overlooking the little courtyard with its tiny fish fountain; the image of the Virgin Mary is still there on the wall, just like when she used to smile on that glimmer of freedom of ours—lunch and recreation— squeezed between the two dingy walls of our lessons. Our mouths tasted of licorice, our hands bore stains, Greek verb paradigms, and "life-saving" formulas still indelible, but ridiculous now in their clandestine futility. We would line up at our places, along the pitch-black benches, and peek on our way, with the same slanted vision of chickens, the napkins variously knotted. Before saying our prayers and standing in line, there were long unnecessary rubbings of hands, as if it were freezing cold. In the air weighed a phony atmosphere of solidarity with the college prefects at the moment of the *Deo gratias*: we would speak unctuously with a companion and look into the eyes of our superior with a haughty expression, which translated meant:

"You have nothing against it, right? We're just talking about you. . . ."

The kitchen boy would enter with a new bowl. Then the joke, for fifteen days, was invariable: "What a waste! The college is going to go to rack and ruin. . . ." And the poor boy, who could barely hold it, would laugh without understanding, widening his pitiful face.

Oh, moody and anarchic puberty, tremendous maturity of the instincts. I used to wear my pants very short too, with very short socks, and my sleeves rolled halfway up, à la *Captain Blood*. Like everyone else, I had a few nervous tics, for example the incessant tossing my hair back, like an irresistible colt. —And I felt like a god.

∾

There were few people that Friday evening at the college alumni gathering. The hot and very long solstitial evening conjured up an outgoing atmosphere. Hence, I took aside my most favorite and peculiar Fathers and opened a small council in the college refectory, on the ground floor.

(As always, when I am among priests I felt comfortable and pleasantly thrilled—perhaps it stems from the electricity that seeps from the incessant kneading and rubbing of their hands. . . .

I have always had a strong sympathy for priests, but especially an inexhaustible curiosity. Monks or secular priests, novices or monsignors, bighead theologians or deacons good only at blowing out candles, beardless seminarians or venerable parish priests who have already celebrated their "golden" mass, emaciated friars or plump priors, ascetics or gourmands, jocks or contemplatives; they all carry that fluid made of a certain *je ne sais quoi* pouring out from the folds of their robes that you instantly know when one of them is around, be it in a tram or a waiting room, creating a special, unique atmosphere.

I love priests. I believe that in any country where I am at night, even in the most remote and inhospitable, there is always a chaste man, whom I do not know and who does not know me, willing to jump out of bed, open up a little door of the rectory, and find an answer to all those bizarre and murky questions, which as children our mother would answer, but as grown ups only priests can. Priests: they will have an answer to all our questions about life, even if sometimes they lack experience and barely know any Latin. But they will be there explaining everything to us, holding our hands and saying from time to time, "It'll be all right, my child. . . . " And once they have restored peace in our hearts, they will send us away through that little door saying only: "Praised be Jesus Christ. . . .")

~◡◔

*F*ather "Head-of-the-table," who chaired our little council, was a nice and peaceful man. One of those specimens of plebeian lineage that eventually takes on oddly aristocratic features and traits in religious life. His ecclesiastical face was large with two purple reticles of veins running down his cheeks. And if a skull rested on his desk, as tradition dictates, it would rather be the skull staring at him with relish, optimistically persuading itself that one day it will become plump and ruddy too, just like the reverend Father.

In spite of his complacent features, the good priest began to complain about how things are going in the world: "Christianity is in crisis, my dear friends," he whined. "Our century keeps disregarding virtue and the holy fear of God. Men and women are uncaring, charity slim and scruffy, churches deserted, saints increasingly rare and bland. Religion is so overlooked and neglected that not even heresies arise any longer," whimpered the reverend Father while comforting himself by taking a snuff of tobacco.

"I understand, Father," I said, "that as a disheartened pastor you suffer very much, but it's not my job to find a remedy for the evils you just mentioned; I might score better with regard to heresies. However, let's talk about these serious matters."

"When all is said and done," declared Father "Skinny-bones," "the world has become a frenzied dance hall. Pleasure: that's the idol that has dethroned Christ in our consciences. For this greedy and jovial humanity there is no other salvation than through the seven plagues of Egypt and the withering away through fasting for at least a hundred years, while beating our chests until we've dug a cave."

"Wonderful program," I said, "to cure obesity, hyperuricemia, and gastrohepatitis, but I think that if we want to save Christianity these, reverend Fathers, are ineffective remedies. The fact is, I am not at all convinced that Christ must necessarily be found buried in our misery and suffering."

"Are you by any chance claiming," jumped animatedly Father "Corrugated-brow," "that Christ came down to earth to preach for a second time the doctrines of Epicurus?"

"Epicurus," I replied, "was a short-sighted and depressed bourgeois who wasn't able to give to human beings a single ounce of true enjoyment, but only a few recipes to avoid indigestion along with an irritating theory of stupid atoms bonded together. Only Christ was able to transform earth in a feast of delights."

George Kordis, *The Resurrection*, Private Collection.
Reproduced by courtesy of the artist.

"A peculiar opinion indeed," said Father "Staring-at-the-ceiling." "And what difference do you see between Epicurus and Christ?"

"Quite simply," I replied, "Epicurus and all the other pagan hedonists, those living two thousand years ago and the ones of today, bustle around, trying to distill joy from pleasant things, whereas Christ taught us to find it *in everything*, even in the most problematic and testing circumstances."

"Like what?"

"Death, for example."

Father "Head-of-the-table" asked me to clarify as he paused in mid-air the pinch of tobacco as though holding a bumblebee by its wings.

"'Turn me over, I'm done on this side,'" I said. "Indeed, I've never heard that before Christianity a red-hot gridiron was such a comfortable spot from where one could crack a joke like Saint Lawrence, or that it could get other martyrs all fired up and ready to sing."

"That Christianity keeps providing us with heroic consolations," protested Father "Tapping-fingers-on-the-table," "does not prove, my dear, that Saint Lawrence was a jovial joker, nor that those others were merry minstrels."

"It proves," I said, "that if a sacred melody can stifle a hot iron burning one's flesh, then the Christian spirit is capable of burying an abyss of pain with a shovelful of joy. In other words, the evil in the world will never be crushed by stoicism, but only through the fervent perseverance of joy."

"I must admit, I find it hard to recognize in these theories of yours the religion that I've been serving for fifty years," muttered old "Father-Wrinkles," "I cannot recall one single line of Christian apologetics claiming for Christians other delights than those of the Hereafter."

"There is no doubt," I said, "that there is a strange trick to Christian catechesis: a kind of secret of state. Christianity does indeed act as if it banishes pleasure, but it is also the only one that fully understands happiness and enjoyment. It gives you a miserable brown bag for breakfast telling you to be content with that, and when you open it and bring that insipid gruel to your mouth you realize that it's a cream for connoisseurs. It preaches chastity, but it was Christianity that discovered sexual pleasure in monotonous monogamy. It rants against those who worship the body— *remember that you are dust . . .* —but it is also the only religion that has gone so far as to issue the dogma of the resurrection of the flesh.

"You're messing up with common sense and desecrating what is sacred," retorted "Father-all-purple." "From what

George Kordis, *Christ with Apostles*, Private Collection.
Reproduced by courtesy of the artist.

"you'll find the alabaster vases of the woman of Bethany with the precious ointment, valuable and fragrant, that inebriated the Lord. . . ."

George Kordis, *The Woman of Bethany*, Private Collection.
Reproduced by courtesy of the artist.

you're saying it almost sounds as if Christianity harbors within its precepts a scandalous complicity with sin."

"Sin's got nothing to do with it," I protested. "It is you who have stubbornly associated pleasure with sin as the two sides of the same coin; that's why churches are deserted, charity almost nonexistent, and saints a rarity. It's time," I said, gesturing, "it's time to snatch out of Satan's hands the prerogative of creating and monopolizing pleasure, which has left us only the dark shadows under our eyes and the dreary Lenten ashes. The pleasure-seekers should know that we reject their pagan hedonism, not so much because it would damn our souls, but because among their ranks one experiences pleasure a thousand times less than among ours.

"To their torpid drunkenness," I added, "we do not oppose the sulk of the abstinent, but the divine remedy of our 'Christ-euphoria.'"

There was a visible uproar amid the ranks of my opponents. Disoriented eyes met, while theological memories, pointlessly flipping through invisible pages, tried to retrieve that curious word that no council had ever coined.

"Christ," counterattacked Father "Arms-wide-open," giving voice to the astonishment of all my judges, "would be flabbergasted to hear an eccentric claiming to fight pleasure with pleasure and recommending for Christians everything but penance."

"Christ," I said, "was flabbergasted when they reproached him because he did not require his disciples to fast while those of the Baptist were sucking locusts for lunch and dinner. *The wedding-guests cannot mourn as long as the bridegroom is with them, can they?* (Matthew 9:15). So I ask: does it seem to you that in two thousand years the groom has abandoned us, even just for one single moment?"

"Mere sophistry," hissed Father "Golden-tooth," "good only for those who loaf about and procrastinate their compliance with the austere laws of the gospel."

"In the Gospels," I burst out, "you won't find only iron nails and dusty sandals, but also the water that the Lord, by performing his first miracle, turned into fine wine at Cana, thus preventing a wedding feast from turning sour; you'll find the alabaster vases of the woman of Bethany with the precious ointment, valuable and fragrant, that inebriated the Lord—even if some may still consider it a luxury and affront to charitable institutions; you'll find the music and the dancing in the house of the prodigal son after his return, the ring, the beautiful dresses, and the fattest calf roasting over the fire; you'll find Peter's nets swollen with silver fishes, and the lilies clothed more beautifully than Solomon."

"In short, Reverend Fathers, you'll find a feast of all the senses experiencing everything in a new and innocent gratitude to the Lord of all creation."

By that time, the good Fathers were mute; the only audible reply to the pounding of my blows would come, while I was catching my breath, from the nose of Father "Head-of-the-table," wearily snorting a pinch of snuff from his snuffbox.

"May we ask you for some advice?" he said, winking at his brothers after an enigmatic silence. "If this is how things are, tell me, what is there left for us priests to do? Are you suggesting that we should try to serve the Gospel of Christ with a renewed spirit? . . ."

"Grace has won the battle with the Law," I replied. "There is no more need of officers of the Law, but of promoters of Grace. 'Grace' means to desire the things that the Law made us afraid of. Grace is about finding more pleasure in avoiding sin than committing it. *More pleasure*, do you understand? Preaching about pain to mankind is a waste of time because pain is a discredited myth. No threat will ever stop a sinner because stronger than sin, stronger than hunger and sex, stronger than man and angels there is only joy."

"What should you do?" I added. "*Dazzle* us: arrange processions more beautiful than glittering dancers on glimmering dance floors; forge bells more melodious than the music of Strauss, use incense more fragrant than the finest perfumes. . . ."

These and other wild ideas came to my mind, but the expression on their faces suppressed them all in my throat.

"It would be enough for me," I finally said, like a convict peacefully choosing his last wish, "that you would stop talking about hell. . . ."

"I hope you at least won't deny the existence of hell!" exclaimed alarmingly Father "Eyes-out-of-its-orbits."

"By all means: I believe that hell is a *possible reality* for humanity: it is there, and every human being can end up in it. But personally, I am convinced that God's infinite mercy will never let that happen to anybody. Nor can you refute me on this, because the Church says that, except for Judas, we can assume that no one is damned."

"So for you hell is a great big empty crypt . . ." said humorously Father "Index-stretched-out."

"That's right," I said. "You may find in it only three chaps, eternally bored and furiously playing games with soot-smeared cards: Beelzebub, Judas Iscariot, and a naked, sexless creature with a colorless face representing 'potential' human beings: the candidate par excellence. While from above the great multitude in heaven sings 'Hallelujah!'"

At that point, the angel came into the refectory and interrupted me while timidly taking me by the hand (was I perhaps blabbering?).

"You've finished praying the Rosary," said the angel. "Now go to the chapel and give thanks."

Going up the stairs, now completely in the dark, I reached the chapel in the midst of my good Fathers' silent cassocks.

ABOUT THE AUTHOR

LUIGI SANTUCCI (Milan, 1918–1999) was one of the most important Italian writers and poets of the second half of the twentieth century. He taught in high schools and worked at the Catholic University of Milan. In 1944, Santucci took refuge in Switzerland because of his opposition to the Italian fascist regime. Back in Milan, he was actively involved in the Italian Resistance, and was one of the co-founders of the underground newspaper *L'Uomo*, with poet David Maria Turoldo and others. Among his books translated into English are *Meeting Jesus—A New Way to Christ* (New York, Herder & Herder, 1971), one of the most original treatments of the life of Christ written in the twentieth century, and *Orfeo in Paradise* (New York, Knopf, 1969), winner in 1967 of Italy's prestigious *Premio Campiello*.

ABOUT THE ILLUSTRATOR

GEORGE KORDIS has illustrated over thirty books. He holds a PhD in Theology from the University of Athens, where he taught the Theory and Practice of Iconography. He is a visiting professor at universities worldwide, including Yale and Notre Dame, and has published and exhibited extensively on secular and sacred themes. Kordis views painting as an endeavor that concerns society and the world and *strives to reveal the metamorphosis of our everyday lives* by combining the Byzantine mode of painting with elements from modern artistic movements. He has also painted churches worldwide including the Docheiariou Monastery at the UNESCO World Heritage Site of Mount Athos and six churches in the USA. For more information, visit www.George-KORDIS.com.

LIST OF ILLUSTRATIONS

ABOUT PARACLETE PRESS

Who We Are

PARACLETE PRESS is a publisher of books, recordings, and DVDs on Christian spirituality. Our publishing represents a full expression of Christian belief and practice—from Catholic to Evangelical, from Protestant to Orthodox.

We are the publishing arm of the Community of Jesus, an ecumenical monastic community in the Benedictine tradition. As such, we are uniquely positioned in the marketplace without connection to a large corporation and with informal relationships to many branches and denominations of faith.

What We Are Doing

PARACLETE PRESS BOOKS ● Paraclete publishes books that show the richness and depth of what it means to be Christian. Although Benedictine spirituality is at the heart of all that we do, we publish books that reflect the Christian experience across many cultures, time periods, and houses of worship. We publish books that nourish the vibrant life of the church and its people.

We have several different series, including the best-selling Paraclete Essentials and Paraclete Giants series of classic texts in contemporary English; Voices from the Monastery—men and women monastics writing about living a spiritual life today; award-winning poetry; best-selling gift books for children on the occasions of baptism and first communion; and the Active Prayer Series that brings creativity and liveliness to any life of prayer.

MOUNT TABOR BOOKS • Paraclete's newest series, Mount Tabor Books, focuses on liturgical worship, art and art history, ecumenism, and the first millennium church, and was created in conjunction with the Mount Tabor Ecumenical Centre for Art and Spirituality in Barga, Italy.

PARACLETE RECORDINGS • From Gregorian chant to contemporary American choral works, our recordings celebrate the best of sacred choral music composed through the centuries that create a space for heaven and earth to intersect. Paraclete Recordings is the record label representing the internationally acclaimed choir Gloriæ Dei Cantores, praised for their "rapt and fathomless spiritual intensity" by *American Record Guide*; the Gloriæ Dei Cantores Schola, specializing in the study and performance of Gregorian chant; and the other instrumental artists of the Gloriæ Dei Artes Foundation.

Paraclete Press is also privileged to be the exclusive North American distributor of the recordings of the Monastic Choir of St. Peter's Abbey in Solesmes, France, long considered to be a leading authority on Gregorian chant.

PARACLETE VIDEO ● Our DVDs offer spiritual help, healing, and biblical guidance for a broad range of life issues including grief and loss, marriage, forgiveness, facing death, bullying, addictions, Alzheimer's, and spiritual formation.

Learn more about us at our website:
www.paracletepress.com
or phone us toll-free at 1.800.451.5006

SCAN
TO
READ
MORE